MANUAL 1:

PREPARING FOR THE FUTURE

WILLS, LETTERS, AND ESSENTIAL DOCUMENTS

STEPHANIE OLDS

Printed in the United States of America
First Edition—Second Printing, May 2025

ISBN: 978-1968178086

Ink and Revival Publishing
Virginia, USA

Welcome

Losing a loved one is one of the hardest things we go through in life. When my mother passed away, I was overwhelmed with grief. But because she had planned ahead, I was able to focus on my emotions and my family instead of scrambling to figure out what needed to be done. Her preparation saved me from so much stress, and I want to help others experience that same peace of mind.

I know that thinking about funeral planning isn't easy. It's one of those things we often put off, hoping we won't have to deal with it anytime soon. But the truth is, making these decisions now can make a world of difference later. When the time comes, your loved ones will be grieving,and having a plan in place will lift a huge burden from their shoulders.

This guide is here to help you take those important first steps. It will walk you through the basics— how to create a will, what documents to organize, and how to leave clear instructions for your family. You don't have to do everything at once, but each step you take now is a gift to your loved ones in the future.

Thank you for taking the time to preparefor something so important. I hope this guide makes the process easier for you and your family.

WHAT'S INSIDE

- ✓ **Why Planning Ahead Matters** – Avoiding confusion, protecting loved ones, and ensuring wishes are honored.

- ✓ **The Importance of a Will** – What a will does, what happens without one, and how to create a simple will.

- ✓ **A Letter to Your Family** – What to include (funeral wishes, account details, passwords, special messages).

- ✓ **Important Documents to Organize** – Birth certificate, insurance policies, property deeds, and bank information.

- ✓ **How to Store Documents Safely** – Fireproof boxes, digital copies, and informing trusted family members.

WHY PREPARING FOR THE FUTURE MATTERS

Thinking about funeral planning is never easy, but avoiding it can leave loved ones with overwhelming stress, unexpected costs, and difficult decisions during an already painful time. The truth is, most families are unprepared. According to the **National Funeral Directors Association (NFDA), as of 2023, nearly 60% of Americans have not discussed their funeral wishes with their family,** and fewer have formal plans in place. This means that, when the time comes, many families are left guessing—often making rushed decisions that may not reflect their loved one's true wishes.

Beyond emotional stress, funeral costs can be a major financial burden. **The average cost of a funeral with burial in 2023 was around $8,000–$10,000,** and prices continue to rise. Without prior planning, families may struggle to cover these expenses, leading to financial strain at an already difficult time.

But it doesn't have to be this way. Taking simple steps now—whether organizing important documents, writing down your wishes, or setting aside funds—can provide peace of mind and ensure that your family isn't left overwhelmed. This guide will walk you through everything you need to know in a clear, step-by-step way. No matter where you are in the planning process, every step you take now is a gift to your loved ones in the future.

Start today. Planning ahead means protecting the people you love.

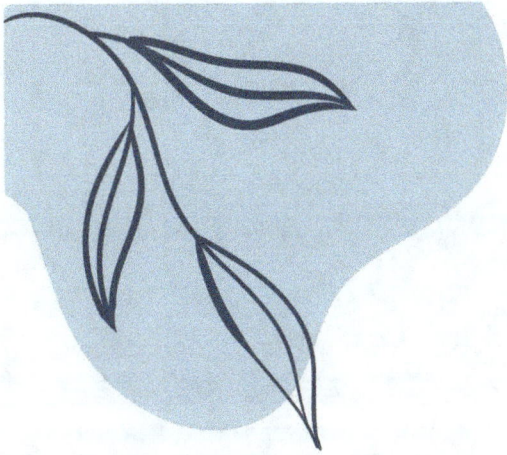

Section 1

Planning Ahead Matters

Why Planning Ahead Matters

Many families struggle with making decisions after a loved one passes away. Without clear instructions, disagreements can arise, and the legal process can become complicated. Planning ahead ensures that your wishes are followed and helps your family avoid unnecessary stress.

Planning ahead is super important, especially when it comes to what happens **_after_** someone passes away. Let's break it down in a simple way.

Imagine if you were going on a big trip. You'd probably want to pack your bags, book your tickets, and plan your activities ahead of time, right? This way, you can enjoy your trip without any last-minute stress. The same idea applies to planning for the future, especially when it comes to important decisions about what happens after someone dies.

When a person plans ahead, they usually create something called a "will." A will is a legal document that says what they want to happen to their things, like their house, money, or special items, after they pass away. According to a survey by Caring.com in 2021, only about 33% of Americans have a will. This means many families might face confusion and disagreements because they don't know what their loved one wanted.

Without a will, the legal process, called "probate," can become complicated and take a long time. Probate is when a court decides how to divide someone's things if they didn't leave clear instructions. This can be stressful and sometimes expensive for families. By planning ahead and having a will, families can avoid these problems and focus on supporting each other during a tough time.

Planning ahead also includes talking to family members about your wishes. This can help prevent disagreements because everyone knows what you want. It's like having a family meeting to decide what movie to watch—everyone gets a say, and you all agree on a plan.

In short, planning ahead is like setting up a roadmap for your family. It helps them know exactly what to do, reduces stress, and makes sure your wishes are respected. It's a thoughtful way to take care of the people you love.

Important Notes, Things to Consider, What to Remember, Immediate Thoughts, Etc.

Important Notes, Things to Consider, What to Remember, Immediate Thoughts, Etc.

Important Notes, Things to Consider, What to Remember, Immediate Thoughts, Etc.

Section 2

Importance of a Will

The Importance of a Will

A **will** is a legal document that states how your property and belongings will be distributed after your death. It also allows you to:

- Name a guardian for minor children.
- Choose an executor (a person who will handle your estate).
- Prevent disputes among family members.

If someone dies without a will (also called **dying intestate**), the state decides how their belongings are divided. This process can take a long time and may not reflect the person's true wishes. Writing a simple will now can prevent these issues.

Let's talk about why having a will is really important. A will is like a special letter that tells everyone what you want to happen to your things after you pass away. Here are some key points about why a will is important:

1. **Deciding Who Gets What:** When you write a will, you can decide who gets your belongings, like your house, money, or even your favorite book collection. Without a will, the state decides, and it might not be what you wanted.

2. **Naming a Guardian for Kids**: If you have children who are under 18, a will lets you choose someone you trust to take care of them if something happens to you. This person is called a guardian.

3. **Choosing an Executor:** An executor is someone you pick to make sure everything in your will is done correctly. They help manage your estate, which is all the things you own, and make sure your wishes are followed.

4. **Preventing Family Disputes:** Sometimes, when there isn't a clear plan, family members might argue about who gets what. A will helps prevent these disagreements because it clearly states your wishes.

5. **Avoiding Intestate Succession:** If you don't have a will, it's called dying intestate. This means the state has rules about who gets your things, and it might take a long time to sort everything out. Plus, it might not match what you would have wanted.

Writing a will doesn't have to be complicated. You can even find simple templates online or get help from a lawyer to make sure everything is done right. It's a good way to make sure your wishes are known and to help your family avoid extra stress during a tough time.

Example Will

Here's an example of what a will for John Doe might look like. Remember, this is a simplified version to help you understand the concept:

Last Will and Testament of John Doe

I, John Doe, residing at [*Your Address*], being of sound mind and body, declare this to be my Last Will and Testament. I revoke all previous wills and codicils made by me.

1. Executor

I appoint my wife, Jane Doe, as the Executor of my will. If she is unable or unwilling to serve, I appoint my friend, [*Friend's Name*], as the alternate Executor.

2. Guardian for Minor Children

If my wife, Jane Doe, is unable to care for our children, I appoint [*Guardian's Name*] as the guardian of my minor children, Joe Doe, Jill Doe, and Jack Doe.

3. Specific Bequests

- I leave my house located at [House Address] to my wife, Jane Doe.
- I leave my used truck to my son, Jack Doe.
- I leave my prized baseball card collection to my son, Joe Doe.
- I leave my prized set of cooking, baking, and grilling collection to my daughter, Jill Doe.
- I leave my prized set of tools and electronics to my son, Jack Doe.

4. Residual Estate

I leave the remainder of my estate, including my $200,000 in retirement funds and any other assets not specifically mentioned, to my wife, Jane Doe. This includes our joint checking and savings accounts.

5. Pet Care

I request that my golden retriever, [*Dog's Name*], be cared for by my family, and I leave $5,000 for the care and maintenance of [*Dog's Name*].

6. Debts and Expenses

I direct that all my just debts, funeral expenses, and costs of administering my estate be paid as soon as practicable after my death.

7. Dispute Resolution

I request that any disputes regarding my will be resolved through mediation before any court proceedings.

8. Signatures

In witness whereof, I have signed this will on [*Date*].

Signature: John Doe	Witness: Witness Name	Witness: Witness Name
John Doe Signature	Witness Signature	Witness Signature

Disclaimer: This example includes key elements like appointing an executor, naming a guardian for minor children, specific bequests, and instructions for handling debts and disputes. It's important to consult with a legal professional when creating a will to ensure it meets all legal requirements..

Practice Will, Things to Consider, What to Remember, Immediate Thoughts, Etc.

Practice Will, Things to Consider, What to Remember, Immediate Thoughts, Etc.

Practice Will, Things to Consider, What to Remember, Immediate Thoughts, Etc.

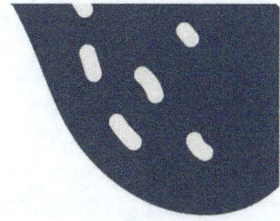

Section 3

Letter to Your Family

A Letter to Your Family

While a will handles legal matters, a personal letter provides important details that aren't covered in legal documents. This letter can include:

- Funeral preferences (burial or cremation, service details, music, readings).
- Account information (bank accounts, insurance policies, debts).
- Online accounts (social media, email, streaming services).
- Special messages to loved ones.

Writing a letter to your family is a thoughtful way to share personal wishes and important information that might not be included in a legal will. This letter can be a comforting guide for your loved ones during a difficult time. Here's why it's important and what it can include:

1. **Funeral Preferences:** You can specify whether you prefer burial or cremation, and share any details about the kind of service you'd like. For example, you might want a particular song played or a specific reading included. This helps your family honor your wishes and can make the planning process easier for them.

2. **Account Information:** Listing your bank accounts, insurance policies, and any debts can save your family a lot of time and stress. It ensures they know where to find important financial information and can help them manage your affairs more smoothly.

3. **Online Accounts:** In today's digital age, many people have numerous online accounts. You can provide login information for social media, email, and streaming services. This helps your family manage or close these accounts, preserving your digital legacy or ensuring your privacy.

4. **Special Messages to Loved Ones:** A personal letter is a wonderful opportunity to leave special messages for your family and friends. You can express your love, share memories, or offer advice. These words can be a source of comfort and connection for your loved ones.

By writing this letter, you're giving your family a gift of clarity and peace of mind. It's a way to show your care and thoughtfulness, even when you're not there to guide them in person.

Example Letter

Here's an example of what a personal letter from John Doe to his family might look like. This letter is meant to provide guidance and share personal messages that aren't typically included in a legal will.

Letter To My Family

Dear Jane, Joe, Jill, and Jack,

If you're reading this, it means I've moved on to the next adventure. I want you all to know how much I love you and how grateful I am for the time we've spent together. I hope this letter helps make things a little easier during this difficult time.

Funeral Preferences:
I would like to be cremated and have my ashes scattered at our favorite family camping spot by the lake. Please keep the service simple and filled with love. I'd love for "*Here Comes the Sun*" by The Beatles to be played, and if someone could read "*The Road Not Taken*" by Robert Frost, that would be wonderful.

Account Information:
- ✓ Our joint checking and savings accounts are with First National Bank. The account numbers are in the safe.
- ✓ My retirement account is with Secure Future Investments. Jane, you should have all the login details.
- ✓ I have a life insurance policy with Family First Insurance. The policy number is in the file cabinet.

Online Accounts:
- ✓ My email is johndoe@email.com. The password is in the safe.
- ✓ My Facebook and Instagram accounts can be accessed with the same email. Feel free to post a message to let friends know.
- ✓ For streaming services like Netflix and Spotify, the login details are saved on my laptop.

Special Messages:
- ➤ Jane, you have been my rock and my greatest love. Thank you for sharing this journey with me. Please take care of yourself and remember to lean on the kids when you need to.
- ➤ Joe, I'm so proud of the man you've become. Keep chasing your dreams and take good care of the baseball card collection. I know you'll appreciate it as much as I did.
- ➤ Jill, your creativity and kindness light up the world. I hope the cooking, baking, and grilling collection inspires you to create wonderful meals and memories.
- ➤ Jack, your curiosity and passion for learning are incredible. The tools and electronics are yours to explore and innovate with. I know you'll do amazing things.

Lastly, please give our golden retriever, Buddy, lots of love and treats. He's been a loyal friend to us all. Take care of each other and remember that I'll always be with you in spirit.

With all my love,
John

This letter is a way for John to express his wishes and share personal messages with his family, providing them with guidance and comfort.

Practice Letter, Things to Consider, What to Remember, Immediate Thoughts, Etc.

Practice Letter, Things to Consider, What to Remember, Immediate Thoughts, Etc.

Practice Letter, Things to Consider, What to Remember, Immediate Thoughts, Etc.

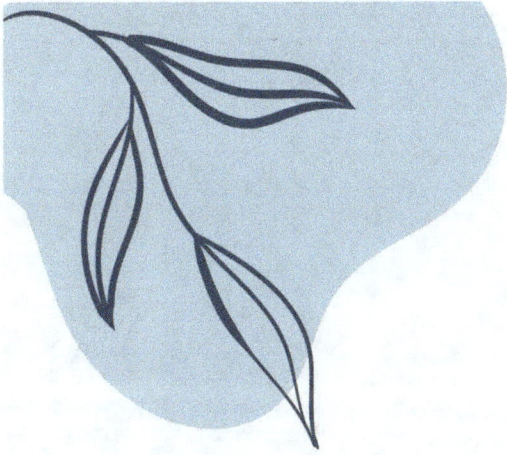

Section 4

Important Documents

Important Documents to Organize

Families often struggle to find key documents after a loved one passes. Keeping these papers in one place can save time and stress:

- Birth and marriage certificates.
- Social Security card.
- Insurance policies.
- Bank and retirement account information.
- Property deeds and vehicle titles.
- Military records (if applicable).

Organizing important documents is a great way to help your family when you're no longer around. Let's look at some key documents you should keep together:

1. **Birth and Marriage Certificates:** These documents prove your identity and relationships. They are often needed for legal processes and benefits.

2. **Social Security Card:** This card is crucial for accessing benefits and handling financial matters. It's important to keep it safe and accessible.

3. **Insurance Policies:** Whether it's life, health, or property insurance, having these documents handy ensures that your family can quickly access the benefits.

4. **Bank and Retirement Account Information:** Details about your accounts help your family manage finances and access funds. This includes account numbers and contact information for financial institutions.

5. **Property Deeds and Vehicle Titles:** These documents prove ownership of your home and vehicles. They are necessary for transferring ownership or selling these assets.

6. **Military Records (if applicable):** If you served in the military, these records can be important for accessing veteran benefits and honors.

By keeping these documents organized and in a safe place, you make it easier for your family to handle important matters. It's also a good idea to let a trusted family member or friend know where these documents are stored. This way, they can find them when needed, reducing stress and confusion during a difficult time.

Important Notes, Things to Consider, What to Remember, Immediate Thoughts, Etc.

Important Notes, Things to Consider, What to Remember, Immediate Thoughts, Etc.

Important Notes, Things to Consider, What to Remember, Immediate Thoughts, Etc.

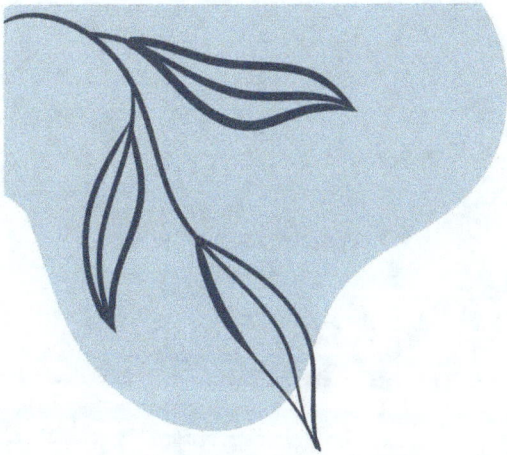

Section 5

Storing Documents

How to Store Documents Safely

Important documents should be kept in a secure but accessible place, such as:

- A **fireproof safe** at home.
- A **safe deposit box** (but make sure a trusted family member can access it).
- A **digital storage service** (scanned copies with password protection).

Having a trusted family member or attorney know where these documents are can prevent confusion when the time comes.

Storing important documents safely is crucial to ensure they are protected from damage and easily accessible when needed. Here are some ways to keep your documents secure:

1. **Fireproof Safe at Home:** A fireproof safe is a great option for storing documents like birth certificates, passports, and insurance policies. These safes are designed to withstand high temperatures, protecting your papers from fire damage. Make sure to choose a safe that is also waterproof to guard against flooding.

2. **Safe Deposit Box:** Many people use safe deposit boxes at banks to store valuable documents. These boxes are secure and protected by the bank's security systems. However, it's important to ensure that a trusted family member or attorney has access to the box, especially in case of emergencies.

3. **Digital Storage Service:** Scanning your documents and storing them digitally is another effective method. You can use cloud storage services like Google Drive, Dropbox, or OneDrive to keep digital copies. Make sure these files are password-protected and that you use strong, unique passwords to keep them secure.

4. **Informing a Trusted Person:** It's essential to let a trusted family member or attorney know where your documents are stored. This can prevent confusion and ensure that your documents are easily accessible when needed.

By taking these steps, you can help protect your important documents and make sure they are available when your family needs them.

Important Notes, Things to Consider, What to Remember, Immediate Thoughts, Etc.

Important Notes, Things to Consider, What to Remember, Immediate Thoughts, Etc.

Important Notes, Things to Consider, What to Remember, Immediate Thoughts, Etc.